Quotations are taken from *St. Francis of Assisi: Writings and Early Documents: English Omnibus f* *the Sources of the Life of St. Francis,* Marion A. Habig, ed., ©1973, used by permission of Franciscan Media. All rights reserved.

Cover and book design by Mark Sullivan

Published by Franciscan Media
28 W. Liberty St.
Cincinnati, OH 45202
www.FranciscanMedia.org

Printed in the United States of America.
Printed on acid-free paper.

If found, please return to:

Let us begin again...

Remember the
words of our Lord,
*Love your enemies, do
good to those who hate you*
(MATTHEW 5:44).

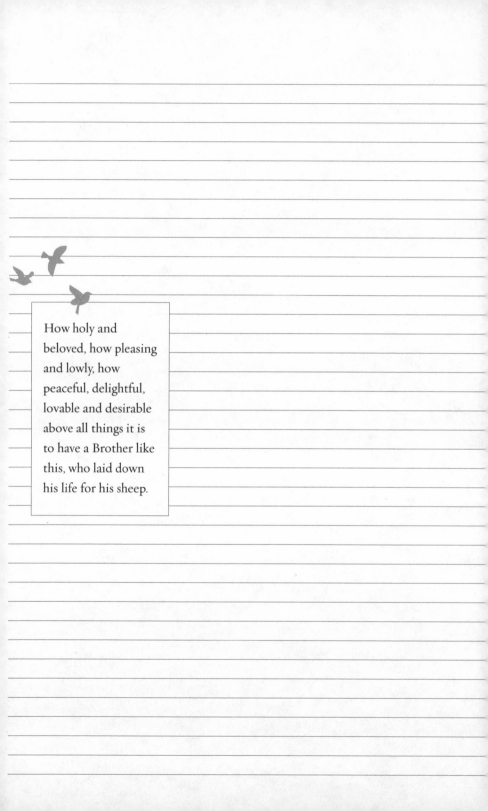

How holy and beloved, how pleasing and lowly, how peaceful, delightful, lovable and desirable above all things it is to have a Brother like this, who laid down his life for his sheep.

We must hate our lower nature with its vices and sins; by living a worldly life, it would deprive us of the love of our Lord Jesus Christ and of eternal life.

In that love which is
God, I entreat all my
friars, ministers and
subjects, to put away
every attachment, all
care and solicitude,
and serve, love,
honor, and adore our
Lord and God with a
pure heart and mind.

We should make a
dwelling place within
ourselves where he
can stay, he who is the
Lord God almighty,
Father, Son, and Holy
Spirit.

Watch, then, praying at all times, that you may be accounted worthy to escape all these things that are to be, and to stand before the Son of Man (LUKE 21:36).

God is spirit, and
they who worship
him must worship in
spirit and truth
(JOHN 4:24).

If you abide in me,
and if my words abide
in you, ask whatever
you will and it shall
be done to you
(JOHN 15:7).

Lord, King of heaven
and earth, we give
you thanks for
yourself. Of your own
holy will you created
all things spiritual
and physical, made
us in your own image
and likeness, and gave
us a place in paradise,
through your only
Son, in the Holy
Spirit.

We should wish for nothing else and have no other desire; we should find no pleasure or delight in anything except in our Creator, Redeemer, and Savior; he alone is true God.

Call no one on earth your father; for one is your Father, who is in heaven. Neither be called masters; for one only is your Master, the Christ who is in heaven (MATTHEW 23:9).

Even as thou hast sent me into the world, so I also have sent them into the world. And for them I sanctify myself, that they also may be sanctified in truth (JOHN 17:19).

We give you thanks because, having created us through your Son, by that holy love with which you loved us, you decreed that he should be born, true God and true man, of the glorious and ever blessed Virgin Mary and redeem us from our captivity by the blood of his passion and death.

We are all poor sinners and unworthy even to mention your name, and so we beg our Lord Jesus Christ, your beloved Son, in whom you are well pleased, and the Holy Spirit, to give you thanks for everything.

At all times and seasons, in every country and place, every day and all day, we must have a true and humble faith.

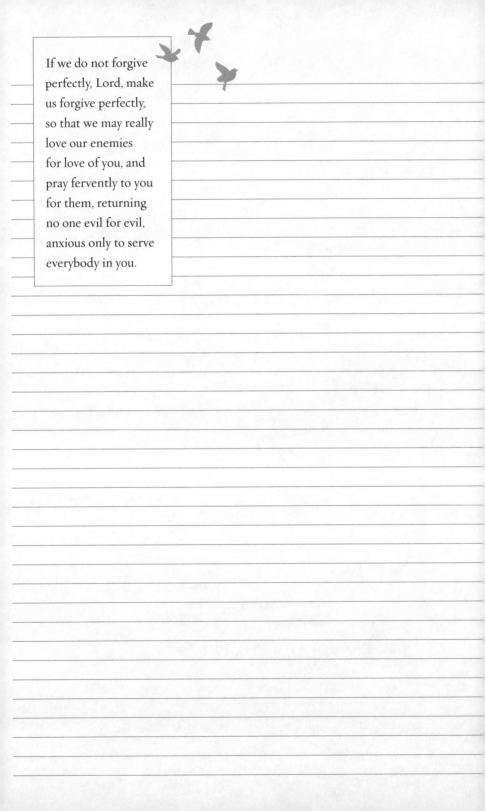

If we do not forgive perfectly, Lord, make us forgive perfectly, so that we may really love our enemies for love of you, and pray fervently to you for them, returning no one evil for evil, anxious only to serve everybody in you.

Let us adore him
with a pure heart for
we must always pray
and not lose heart
(see LUKE 18:1).

Behold I am with
you even unto the
consummation of
the world
(MATTHEW 28: 20).

I pray for them; not for the world do I pray, but for those whom thou hast given me, because they are thine, and all things that are mine are thine (JOHN 17:9).

Our Lord Jesus told his disciples, I am the way, and the truth, and the life. No one comes to the Father but through me.

It is really the Spirit
of God who dwells in
his faithful.

The words that I
have spoken to you
are spirit and life
(JOHN 6:64).

I did not come to be served but to serve (MATTHEW 20:28), our Lord tells us.

We must keep a close watch over ourselves and let nothing tarnish the purity of our senses.

I say to you, my
friends: Do not
be afraid of those
who kill the body,
and after that have
nothing more that
they can do. Take
care that you do not
be alarmed. By your
patience you will win
your souls. He who
has persevered to
the end will be saved
(MATTHEW 10:28).

We must all be on our guard against pride and empty boasting and beware of worldly or natural wisdom. A worldly spirit loves to talk a lot but do nothing, striving for the exterior signs of holiness that people can see, with no desire for true piety and interior holiness of spirit.

Humility, patience,
perfect simplicity,
and true peace of
heart are all its aim,
but above everything
else it desires the
fear of God, the
divine wisdom and
the divine love of the
Father, Son, and Holy
Spirit.

We must refer every good to the most high supreme God, acknowledging that all good belongs to him.

May the most
supreme and high
and only true God
receive and have and
be paid all honor and
reverence, all praise
and blessing, all
thanks and all glory,
for to him belongs
all good and no one
is good but only God
(see LUKE 18:19).

When we see or hear people speaking or doing evil or blaspheming God, we must say and do good, praising God, who is blessed forever.

It is well for those
who die repentant;
they shall have a place
in the kingdom of
heaven.

Sanctify them in truth. Thy word is truth (JOHN 17:17).

Holy Father, keep in thy name those whom thou hast given me, that they may be one even as we are. These things I speak in the world, in order that they may have my joy made full in themselves (see JOHN 15:11).

Almighty, most high
and supreme God,
Father, holy and
just, Lord, King of
heaven and earth, we
give you thanks for
yourself.

Of your own holy will
you created all things
spiritual and physical,
made us in your own
image and likeness,
and gave us a place
in paradise, through
your only Son, in the
Holy Spirit.

We give you thanks because, having created us through your Son, by that holy love with which you loved us, you decreed that he should be born, true God and true man, of the glorious and ever blessed Virgin Mary and redeem us from our captivity by the blood of his passion and death.

We Friars Minor, servants and worthless as we are, humbly beg and implore everyone to persevere in the true faith and in a life of penance; there is no other way to be saved.

With all our hearts
and all our souls, all
our minds and all
our strength, all our
power and all our
understanding, with
every faculty and
every effort, with
every affection and
all our emotions, with
every wish and desire,
we should love our
Lord and God.

We should find no
pleasure or delight
in anything except
in our Creator,
Redeemer, and
Savior; he alone is
true God.

I am the way, and the
truth, and the life
(JOHN 14:6).

May the power of your love, O Lord, fiery and sweet as honey, wean my heart from all that is under heaven, so that I may die for love of your love, you who were so good as to die for love of my love.

Blessed are those
who suffer
persecution for
justice's sake,
for theirs is the
kingdom of heaven
(MATTHEW 5:10).
He who has
persevered to the end
will be saved.

When I was in sin,
the sight of lepers
nauseated me beyond
measure; but then
God himself led me
into their company,
and I had pity on
them.

And God inspired
me with such faith
in his churches that
I used to pray with
all simplicity, saying,
"We adore you, Lord
Jesus Christ, here and
in all your churches in
the whole world, and
we bless you, because
by your holy cross you
have redeemed the
world."

The Most High himself made it clear to me that I must live the life of the Gospel.

Those who do not
know how to work
should learn, not
because they want
to get something for
their efforts, but to
give good example
and to avoid idleness.

> God revealed a form
> of greeting to me,
> telling me that we
> should say, "God give
> you peace."

And so it is really the Spirit of God who dwells in his faithful who receive the most holy Body and Blood of our Lord. Anyone who does not have this Spirit and presumes to receive him eats and drinks judgement to himself.

How long will you be dull of heart? Why do you refuse to recognize the truth and believe in the Son of God? Every day he humbles himself just as he did when he came from his heavenly throne.

It is the Most High himself who has told us,

This is my Body and Blood of the new covenant and He who eats my flesh and drinks my blood has life everlasting.

We, too, with our own eyes, see only bread and wine, but we must see further and firmly believe that this is his most holy Body and Blood, living and true.

Try to realize the dignity God has conferred on you. He created and formed your body in the image of his beloved Son, and your soul in his own likeness.

> Look at the Good Shepherd, my brothers. To save his sheep he endured the agony of the cross.

We can never tell
how patient or
humble a person is
when everything is
going well with him.
But when those who
should cooperate
with him do the exact
opposite, then we
can tell. A man has as
much patience and
humility as he has
then, and no more.

A person is really
poor in spirit when
he hates himself and
loves those who strike
him in the face.

> Blessed are the
> peacemakers, for
> they shall be called
> the children of God
> (MATTHEW 5:9).

Blessed are the clean
of heart, for they shall
see God (MATTHEW
5:8).

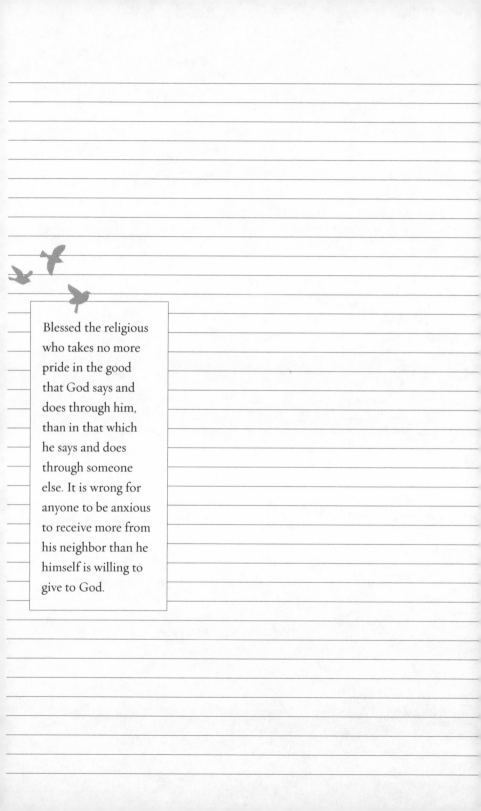

Blessed the religious
who takes no more
pride in the good
that God says and
does through him,
than in that which
he says and does
through someone
else. It is wrong for
anyone to be anxious
to receive more from
his neighbor than he
himself is willing to
give to God.

Blessed the man
who is patient
with his neighbor's
shortcomings as he
would like him to be
if he were in a similar
position himself.

Where there is Love and Wisdom, there is neither Fear nor Ignorance.

I am the servant of all and so I am bound to wait upon everyone and make known to them the fragrant words of my Lord.

Our Lord Jesus
Christ is the glorious
Word of the Father,
so holy and exalted.

Those who love God are happy and blessed. They do as our Lord himself tells us in the Gospel, *Thou shalt love the Lord thy God with thy whole heart, and with thy whole soul, ...and thy neighbor as thyself.*

We must love God... and adore him with a pure heart and mind, because this is what he seeks above all else.

> True worshippers will worship the Father in spirit and in truth.

We should praise him
and pray to him day
and night, saying,
*Our Father, who art in
heaven,* because we
must always pray and
not lose heart.

We must be
charitable, too, and
humble, and give
alms, because they
wash the stains of sin
from our souls.

We lose everything
which we leave
behind us in this
world; we can bring
with us only the
right to a reward for
our charity and the
alms we have given.
For these we shall
receive a reward, a
just retribution from
God.

How glorious, how holy and wonderful it is to have a Father in heaven.

Holy Father, in your
name keep those
whom you have given
me. Father, all those
whom you gave me in
the world, were yours
and you gave them to
me. And the words
you have given me, I
have given to them
(JOHN 6:39).

Father, I wish that where I am, they also may be with me, that they may see my splendor in your kingdom (JOHN 17:24).

Every creature in
heaven and on earth
and in the depths
of the sea should
give God praise and
glory and honor and
blessing.

All those who refuse to do penance and receive the Body and Blood of our Lord Jesus Christ are blind, because they cannot see the true light, our Lord Jesus Christ.

Kissing your feet
with all the love I am
capable of, I beg you
to show the greatest
possible reverence
and honor for the
most holy Body and
Blood of our Lord
Jesus Christ through
whom all things,
whether on the earth
or in the heavens,
have been brought to
peace and reconciled
with Almighty God.

He who is of God
hears the words of
God.

Almighty, eternal,
just and merciful
God, grant us in our
misery that we may
do for your sake alone
what we know you
want us to do.

There is one thing of which we can all boast; we can boast of our humiliations and in taking up daily the holy cross of our Lord Jesus Christ.